When I Remember, I Remember When

by

Della Bell Moore

ISBN: 978-1-4269-6630-9 (sc)
ISBN: 978-1-4269-6631-6 (hc)
ISBN: 978-1-4269-6632-3 (e)

Library of Congress Control Number: 2011908488

Trafford rev. 05/25/2011

 www.trafford.com

North America & international
toll-free: 1 888 232 4444 (USA & Canada)
phone: 250 383 6864 ✦ fax: 812 355 4082

In Memory of my parents, Clyde and Marie Bell, who made me what I am today and gave me so many wonderful happy memories.

TABLE OF CONTENTS

WAR TIME

*W*hen I remember I remember when my Father was away during World War II. My Mother and I stayed with my Grandmother and Great Grandparents and they looked after me while my Mom worked at the Industrial Rayon Plant in Covington, Virginia. The plant made nylon cord which was used for parachutes. My Mom's picture was in the newspaper with an article about her being one of the top operators in the plant. My Daddy was in the 101st Airborne and I've often wondered since I grew up if some of the nylon which Mom helped make could have been used in a parachute which helped bring him safely down on his jumps.

I remember going with my Mom back and forth on the C&O train or Greyhound bus from Covington, Virginia to Ft. Bragg, North Carolina to see my Dad before he was shipped out. The buses and trains were always packed with people standing. Most of the passengers were in uniform. I remember soldiers and sailors holding me on their laps for hours. I didn't realize that Mom knew most of them since they were boys she had grown up with.

I remember missing a connecting bus somewhere in North Carolina and spending the rest of the night in the bus station.

I remember a friend Mom made while we were in Ft. Bragg. Her husband was also stationed at the base. Mrs. LaPoe was from Holland, Michigan. She took care of me when Mom was sick.

She fed me Ritz crackers with grape jelly on them. To this day it is one of my favorite snacks.

I remember my Dad's oldest brother got home from overseas before my Dad did. Uncle Leroy wasn't married and had no children so every Friday night he came to my Grandparents and picked me up to go to the movies. They were in black and white of course and always westerns.....Tom Mix, Gene Autry and the King of the Cowboys, Roy Rogers. How I looked forward to those Friday nights!

I remember Mom tracing the outline of my hand on paper to mail to Daddy so he could see how big I was getting.

When I was four years old I had a WAC suit complete with hat and handbag. Mom took me to Miller's Studio in Covington to have pictures made to mail to Daddy. It got packed away and forgotten when my two girls were four years old. It was found after my Grandmother passed away, but minus the hat and handbag. We have no idea what happened to them. I have pictures of both my Granddaughters in that suit when they were each four years old. And just recently we took a picture of my almost four year old Great Granddaughter in the suit. We have several other Great Granddaughters now and when they reach four we will take their pictures in my little WAC suit.

Author's Mother, Marie Bell, during World War II doffing spools of nylon cord to be used in making parachutes among other articles to be used in the War effort.

Leroy Bell, author's uncle, took her to the movies every Friday night after he got home from the War until her Father was discharged.

Jessica Shifflett, Della Bell Moore, Amy Moore

Author at four years of age (middle photo), Granddaughter Jessica Shifflett, four years old on left and Granddaughter Amy Moore, four years old on right in the same WAC suit.

MY ONLY PUPPY

*W*hen I remember, I remember when my Dad came home from World War II. We moved from Covington, Va. to Richmond, Va. for about a year so he could go to barber school on the GI bill. We rented a little cottage on Midlothian Turnpike in the style popular at that time and the forerunner of the modern day motel. There were large trees all around the different units and being an only child I was use to entertaining myself and had a vivid imagination. I played many games of cowboys and Indians around those trees taking the parts of both sides.

During the time we lived there someone gave Daddy a puppy for me. He was a little black and white mixed breed. My parents never believed in having animals in the house so when evening came the first day my Dad fixed a little pen for the puppy next to our cabin. He barked just a little, but quickly settled in and was quiet all night. But the next morning when we went outside the puppy was gone. We didn't know if he had run off or if someone had taken him. My dad put me in the car and we went up and down Midlothian Turnpike hunting for my dog, but we never found him. Daddy asked everyone he saw out walking, but no one had seen him.

I never had another dog of my own.

UNDERSHIRTS

When I remember, I remember when I was in second grade. Moma would still make me wear an undershirt to school to keep my chest warm so I wouldn't catch cold. (In her defense I had whooping cough in first grade, missed six weeks of school and almost died so she was really protective.) I don't think you could see the undershirt beneath my outer clothing, but I knew it was there and I was positive I was the only girl in second grade who had to wear one. So I would go to the restroom as soon as I got to school in the morning, undress and take the undershirt off and stuff it into my book bag. When school was out for the day I would run to the restroom and put the undershirt back on before walking home. I don't ever remember being caught doing that, but by third grade I was big enough I didn't have to wear an undershirt anymore.

WEEPING WILLOW TREE

When I remember, I remember when my Great Grandparents lived in an old two story house that had once been the Methodist church parsonage and had been pulled to the present location by horses approximately one/half mile through a creek. My Grandma loved flowers and the yard was completely filled with plants of all kinds. Heaven help the Grandchild who threw a ball or ran through her flowers. You had a timeout on the back porch where she sat with a switch across her lap to be sure you didn't move. But I always knew it was spring when her hyacinths bloomed.

One of our favorite games when my cousins came was to get an old peanut butter or similar jar, punch some holes in the lid and see who could catch the most bees without getting stung. The big bumblebees were the easiest to catch. We would always turn them loose later.

She also had a huge weeping willow tree in the front yard. I spent many happy hours playing house under that tree. I would outline the rooms with small gravel from the driveway leaving blank spaces for the doors and windows. My dolls and I would play for hours and have our tea parties. The branches hung to the ground so if you were quiet and still no one could really see you.

Every time my husband and I have moved through the years I have always said I wanted to plant a weeping willow tree. No luck so far, but maybe......where we live now.

The author's Grandparents home after the brick look alike siding had been installed to help the looks and also help keep the cold from coming through the cracks in the winter. You can barely see the weeping willow tree in the left hand corner of the picture.

BUTTER MAKING

*W*hen I remember, I remember when we went to my Grandmother Bells and I helped her make butter. Ma Bell would milk the cow (with a little help from me) and then we would separate the milk from the cream. The milk was poured into a container on the separator. Then a hand crank was turned and the cream came out one holder and the milk came out another. I loved to turn the crank. Since this was before Grandma had an icebox or refrigerator the milk was placed in the springhouse to keep cool. Grandma would use the cream to make butter or cottage cheese. I don't remember how she made the cottage cheese, but my Mom always said it was the best cottage cheese in the world. I remember making the butter in the old wooden churn. It was fun making the paddle go up and down at first, but became work as the mixture became thicker and harder to make the paddle move. I'm sure it didn't take long for my arms to give out and Grandma would have to finish the job.

I remember during the war when we were staying at my Grandma Alfreds and she would get her ration of oleo (butter/margarine). It came in a square of white grease which looked exactly like lard and not at all appetizing. There would be a little packet of yellow powder with the oleo. My Grandma Jo would dump everything into a big bowl and mix the coloring in with her hands. It didn't change the taste, but certainly looked a lot better. And then we had butter to go with our biscuits for the next few days.

CHURCH HATS AND TOPPERS

*W*hen I remember, I remember when no self respecting lady or young girl would go to church without a hat. If you had enough money you could buy hats in different colors to complement your clothes, but most everyone I knew had two hats. A white hat we wore all summer and a black hat we wore all winter. The same with our shoes, white after Memorial Day and black after Labor Day. (I still have problems seeing white shoes in the winter time.) If we were really lucky we also had gloves to match.

I remember my favorite white hat fit close to my head and had a long white feather which hung over the top of the hat attached to a little veil. My black hat was a little larger with a medium brim and a red rose was attached to that. You could take the flower off and add one of a different color so that made it seem like a new hat at times.

Easter was of course the major event of the spring. We would make a corsage from Grandma's hyacinths or daffodils and pin that to our new spring topper. The weather in the mountains of Virginia was still cool enough at Easter that you needed a wrap. The topper was a ½ or ¾ length light weight coat which usually came in beautiful pastel colors.

Oh, how prissy and sweet we pre-teens and teenagers looked on our way to Sunday School.

FISHING

When I remember, I remember when my Dad went fishing in a little stream near my Grandma and Granddaddy Bell's house in Craig County, Virginia. He caught several trout and hooked them on a little twig to carry back to the house. Daddy and Mom were walking down the little graveled road and I was running on ahead of them. I was carrying the fish so I could show them off. I decided to stop and wash them first. I got in the middle of the stream standing on some rocks and dipped the branch in the water. The current was so strong it immediately pulled the twig out of my hand down stream and I couldn't catch it. Daddy was too far behind me to catch it so we didn't have fish for supper.

I never remember him going fishing again. At least not with me.

FIRED

When I remember, I remember when I was helping my Dad fix the roof on our house. The roof was not very steep and I had no problem being up there. The only thing was that last step off the ladder onto the roof and the first step from the roof back onto the ladder.

I do not remember what the disagreement was about, but Daddy and I started arguing. The next door neighbor was mowing his yard right at the fence line just then and he called up to my Dad and said, "Clyde, are you going to fire that girl?" I answered him back and said "No, I'm going to quit." And down off the roof onto the ladder I went.

My Dad came down right behind me laughing so hard he could hardly see. I went into the house and fixed him a cup of coffee and got myself a cold drink. We set on the porch until we cooled off, then back up on the roof to finish the repair job.

Daddy never minded me "talking back" as long as I did what he wanted me to do in the first place. I inherited my quick answers (for good and bad) from him.

SHE

$\mathcal{W}$hen I remember, I remember when my Great Grandmother was alive. From my earliest memories she was a tall, big boned woman with a care lined face, her hair almost entirely grey and her faded blue eyes, wise and serene, as if she had seen all the happiness and sorrow which life had to offer and yet was untouched by it.

I didn't know much about her then, only that she was hard working and believed fiercely that children should be seen and not heard. The only time we got along was when I would help her in the garden or run errands to the neighbors or store for her and then I would demand pay. A nickel for a Nehi grape soda or a dime for that and a candy bar. When I wanted to play she wanted me to set on a chair and be quiet and that resulted in many screams and tears, always on my part.

She would rather work outside than inside any time. She always had a large garden and a good crop. She loved to can and many of her vegetables from the garden and fruit from the trees planted in her yard found its way into the rows and rows of jars which were stored in the cellar. I never remember the cellar unless it was packed to capacity because only after a year of eating and giving away was there the slightest sign of decrease and by then it was gardening and canning time again.

She was never happier than when she had company and she would stand for hours uncomplaining over the wood stove on the hottest days and prepare huge platters of meat and many other good dishes. My favorites were her jelly cake, six thin layers with jelly in between each one and powdered sugar on the top and fresh banana cake which had to be eaten right away before the fruit turned brown. Her table was loaded with jams and jellies of all kinds which she made each summer. If she didn't grow the fruit she would buy it so we always had a variety. Even though her home was a dilapidated old farmhouse everyone who came in left feeling as if they had been royally entertained.

She loved pretty things, silks and satins and laces, embroidery, crochet, knitting and quilting. She quilted every winter until her eyesight became too dim to see the fine stitches required. Her quilts are highly valued today and everyone who sees them exclaims over their beauty. She loved red and almost all her descendants love that color also.

She loved the church and attended services regularly when her health permitted. She was a great worker in the church and was a charter member along with her husband. Whenever the traveling evangelists came through that part of the country they stayed at her home.

She was always called upon when there was sickness or death for miles around. She washed and dressed the bodies for burial and placed new pennies on the eyes of the deceased to keep them shut. She nursed many children through the whooping cough, measles and mumps. The Doctor said I would have died had she not nursed me thru whooping cough. I remember coughing until I was out of breath and would have to lay down on the floor until I could breathe again. I was six years old at the time.

She had a large family, eight children, so she stayed close to home for many years. After the children were all grown she loved to visit other friends and family members.

When she was gone we always missed her, but we always thought she would be back. And yet, one bleak March morning became even bleaker when the friend she was visiting at the time called and said she had passed away.

All during the lonely days, weeks, months and years now since she has been gone I have visited her grave many times and placed flowers on it every season of the year. I realize now what I didn't know then, the love in her heart and the wisdom in her eyes could have been mine had I only sat and listened when she wanted to talk.

Yes, she's gone, my Great Grandmother, but often when I'm troubled and mixed up I wish I could have her back to talk to and have her help me solve my problems. In that beautiful old gray head were answers to many things that trouble me. The memories of her will always be with me and someday I will share them with my children and my children's children.

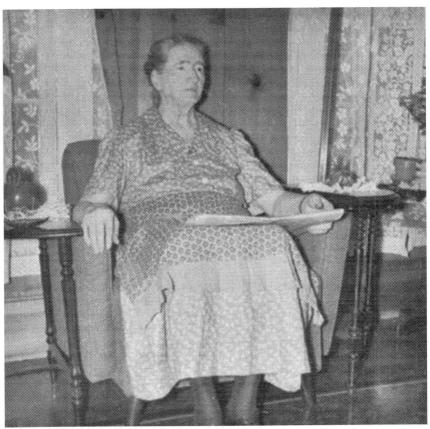

Author's Great Grandmother, Linnie Viola McDaniel Alfred. Not all of the cousins have good memories of her and her strict ways.

DR. PEPPER MAN

When I remember I remember when there was a local contest going on sponsored by Dr. Pepper soft drink. If the Dr. Pepper man came to your house he would give you a silver dollar for each bottle of Dr. Pepper you had on hand up to twelve dollars. My Grandma Alfred bought two six packs of Dr. Pepper and put them away out of sight just in case. And the Dr. Pepper man did come, not only once, but several times. The old house was so dilapidated I guess he thought the people who lived there needed the money more than anyone else in the neighborhood.

Only one time really stands out in my memory. A cousin and I had been doing some yard work for Grandma. She usually would give us a nickel or dime and we would go down to the store and get a soda pop or candy bar. I don't remember why, but that day she must have been slow giving us the money and we were too thirsty to wait. So, yes, we went and got two bottles out of the six pack. Sure enough the Dr. Pepper man knocked on the front door. My Grandma thought she had another twelve dollars, but actually only received ten.

That's the only time I remember taking her Dr. Pepper.

I never did know what she did with the silver dollars she won.

FIGHTING CLOTHES

When I remember I remember when I was growing up we stayed with my Great Grandmother (Grandma Alfred) and Great Grandfather (Grandaddy) and Grandma Jo while my Dad was in World War II. I have many stories about them, but my favorite about Grandma is one when her children were small. Apparently one of my uncles was a real stinker. One day someone knocked on the front door and when my Grandma went to answer it was the school marm. "Mrs. Alfred" she said. "I've come to see you about your son Carl and I'm afraid I have my fighting clothes on". My Grandmother stepped back from the door and said "Come in. I keep my fighting clothes on".

There are some in the family even today who think I am a lot like my Grandmother.

GOOSEBERRIES

When I remember I remember when Grandma Alfred had a large family and most of them married and had large families. I was actually a Great Grandchild so by the time I could remember there were a lot of us. I really do have cousins by the dozens. Part of this took place during World War II and much food had to be raised and preserved at home. Grandma was a true caretaker and worked very hard to see that no one went hungry or cold.

She raised a huge garden each year, close to ¾ of an acre. But there were two rows of gooseberry bushes planted the entire width of the garden plot. It was probably close to fifty bushes. Now, gooseberries are delicious to eat when ripe. They can be made into jams, jellies and pies although I never cared for those. But they are hard to pick. The gooseberry vines have stickers on them (thorns) similar to a rose bush. The berries grow under the vine so you have to hold the vine up with one hand and pick the berries off with the other. Like so many things in a garden they all seemed to ripen at one time. I have spent many hours picking gooseberries bending over in the hot sun.

At night after supper we would set on the back porch and cap the berries so they could be eaten or canned. There was a little stem on each side of the berry. You would pinch the stem off between your thumb and forefinger. Your fingers would be sore and a little stained by the time you pinched what seemed like a million stems.

The old home place has one gooseberry vine left and most years it does not produce much fruit. And no one today wants to fool with it and pick what is there. I transplanted two bushes to my own home and have moved them four times now. I always know my birthday is close when the berries ripen in mid-June.

I just pick them, eat and enjoy. What I don't get the birds do.

HOBOS

When I remember I remember when times were hard after the war and men everywhere were losing their jobs. Many left their homes and wandered from place to place looking for work. For the most part they were honest and hard working, just poor. The ones who hopped freight trains from town to town were usually called hobos while those who walked the highways were called tramps.

My grandparents lived in one of the poorer looking houses on old Route 60 in western Virginia. Their house had once been the Methodist church parsonage and had been moved from its former location across a creek on a pole sled of some sort pulled by a team of horses to the present location where they lived.

Every tramp and hobo who came through that part of Virginia stopped at their house for a handout and were never turned down. My Grandmother wouldn't let them in the kitchen, but made them set on the porch and eat. She would set where she could watch them. She fed them well and they could have all the cool water they wanted to drink from the hand pump on the back porch.

The author's Grandparents old house before the fake looking brick siding was installed. Since the picture was taken in the winter you cannot see the weeping willow tree, but it is in the right hand side of the picture.

PANTYHOSE

When I remember I remember when there was no such thing as pantyhose. Hose came in pairs, one for each leg. You held them up with either a girdle or garter belt, under garments which had small pieces of elastic with hooks on the end to attach to the tops of the hose. You could wear just a garter which was a length of elastic worn above the knee and wrapped two or three times around the hose. Hose had seams in them which were worn in the back and went straight up the middle of the leg. You never wanted to be caught with crooked seams. What fun to get them on and straight in hot weather when they stuck to you every inch. Eventually they made seamless hose so that took care of that problem. Hose were not prepackaged at the store, but you bought them from a box. The clerk would wrap them in tissue paper to keep them from snagging or running. You always bought two pair if you had the money. That way if one hose got a run you had another from the second pair to replace it. That made the purchase go a lot further. You could stop a run by dabbing some clear fingernail polish on the hole. A lady never went bare legged in public. You graduated from anklets to hose. During WWII nylons were among the rationed goods as all the nylon was being used for parachutes for the military.

LIGHTNING BUGS

When I remember I remember when my cousins would come to visit. We would all be at my grandmothers in the summer. After dinner dishes were done the grownups would set on the front porch talking and we kids would be in the yard lying in the grass on our backs looking at the stars and trying to pick out the constellations; the Big Dipper, the Little Dipper and the Milky Way. The grass would be damp with dew and full of little night insects. The smell of Grandma's flowers would be overwhelming in the warm night air. Lightning bugs would be flashing their presence everywhere. We would jump up from the ground to see who could catch the most. We would hold them loosely in our hands and watch the little flashes of light before letting them go. Sometimes we would catch them in the same jars we caught the bees in during the day. Then, Grandma would call, "Time to come in and get washed up for bed". Oh, what simple happy times.

My cousins both had beautiful singing voices and I had none, but I would try to chime in and we would entertain the adults with hymns. I was usually told to hush by my great grandmother so they could hear the others clearly and not be distracted by my off key attempts. To this day I am very self conscious and usually will not sing where others can hear.

READING

When I remember I remember when my Grandma would set in a straight backed kitchen chair and read half the night by the light of a flashlight. Granddaddy didn't want her to waste the newly installed electric power. I love to read and attribute my love of books to her. She taught me to care for my books; don't bend the backs, don't dog ear the pages and don't mark the pages in any way. To this day I cannot stand a book that is messed up. I feel if you can read and comprehend then you can learn anything.

I was actually punished for not coming when called to a meal etc by my Mom not allowing me to bring any library books home for a specified length of time depending on what I was being punished for. I would get a library book and put it inside my Latin book and read all during class. I didn't learn much Latin, but read a lot of books that year. Daddy complained I never saw anything on our trips because every time he looked in the rear view mirror I was reading.

Every yard sale and book store I pass calls my name and I have to stop and see what they have. I probably have a thousand books at home right now and will never live long enough to read them all.

Thank you, Grandma. I go to sleep every night with the lamp on and a book in my hand.

PAPER DOLLS

When I remember I remember when some of my best friends were paper dolls. Books of paper dolls, from baby dolls to grown up paper dolls. Some you had to cut out with scissors and others were perforated so you could punch them out. Clothes for them of all styles from swim suits to evening gowns. Little tabs on the sides of the clothing bent around and held the outfit on the doll. In some cases even accessories, shoes, hats and handbags were included. The dolls were made of lightweight cardboard to make them more durable. Later, they were magnetic so the clothes would stay on without the tabs. Paper doll families were kept in shoe boxes so they wouldn't get torn up or lost. The dolls provided hours and hours of fun.

T.V.

When I remember I remember when I saw my first television. My parents and I were on vacation going from Covington, Virginia to Niagara Falls, New York. We stopped in Pittsburgh, Pennsylvania for lunch at a little diner. They had a small black and white T.V. setting on a shelf on the wall. I was twelve years old and had to crane my neck to see over the side of the booth. The Lone Ranger was playing on the screen. I was so excited I couldn't eat, but I didn't miss a thing on the program. I'm afraid that for me even Niagara Falls took a back seat to the miracle of T.V. on that trip.

I remember baby setting for a couple who had perhaps the first television in our neighborhood. The screen was a circle approximately eight inches in diameter. It was housed in a huge floor model console. I loved to baby set for them.

My aunt and uncle who lived just down the road from us got a T.V. before we did. Most evenings they would call to see if I wanted to come down and watch with them. The first time I saw Elvis Presley was on their T.V.

And finally my parents bought a television. Oh, happy day! The early T.V. sets took five minutes to warm up so you could get a picture. And if one of the tubes blew you would have to take them all to the shop to see which one was bad so you could replace it.

The first item my husband and I purchased after we were married was a television set from Sears Roebuck, 1700 West Broad Street, Richmond, Va. We opened up a charge account and because of our ages, I was eighteen and he was nineteen, we had to have a co-signer. His sister was not allowed to sign for us even though she had a good job as a legal secretary so our brother-in-law co-signed for us. We had that charge account with Sears for probably twenty five years and we were never late with a payment and never missed one.

TIPPY

When I remember I remember when the next door neighbor's dog, Tippy, adopted us as his family although he went back and forth between the two houses. Tippy was a mixed breed, a big black shaggy dog and I loved him dearly. He would run and play with us, follow everywhere we went, go swimming with us in the creek behind the house and lay on our patio in the evenings.

Due to a strike at the Westvaco plant in Covington, Virginia we moved away for a year to Roanoke, Virginia where my Dad opened a barber shop. He had gone to barber school on the GI bill after WWII. My Grandma Jo lived one mile from us in Callaghan around a curve in the road. We came back to her house every Friday and left every Sunday for the entire year we were moved away.

We have no explanation as to how he knew, but every Friday when we got to my Grandma's Tippy would be in her front yard wagging his tail waiting for us. He would spend all day Saturday and stay at her house even if we left for a short time. After our car would pull out of the driveway on Sunday he would head back up the road to his home and my Grandma would not see him again until Friday just before time for us to come again.

After the Westvaco strike was over we moved back next door to Tippy. I remember when he got old and ready to die he came to our house, crawled underneath and went peacefully to sleep.

My Dad went under the house, pulled him out and buried him for the neighbors.

Although Tippy didn't belong to me in the real sense, he belonged to me in that special bond of animal and person.

MILK DELIVERY

When I remember I remember when milk was delivered to your door in glass bottles with cardboard stoppers. You used the milk and set the bottle back on your porch to be picked up the next time the milkman delivered. Usually you got the same number of bottles of milk left as you had empty bottles set out.

My father worked for a dairy in Roanoke, Virginia for a short time when the Westvaco paper mill was on strike in Covington. He had a regular delivery route which went through a poor neighborhood. There was a little boy on his route who would be outside playing and who loved cottage cheese. When he would see my dad coming in the dairy truck he would start hollering "cot cheese, cot cheese". My Dad would stop the truck, take the money out of his pocket, put it in the till and give the little boy a carton of cottage cheese.

I believe Daddy was putting stars in his crown even before he became a Christian.

DROWNED BOY

When I remember I remember when I was about twelve years old. We went swimming almost every day in the summer underneath a railroad bridge where the deepest part of the creek was about twenty five feet. My Mom would get all the housework done in the morning and right after lunch load me and usually a friend or two and a few cousins and we would drive to the swimming hole. We had to park on the side of the road , walk through a cornfield and down a path to the water.

This particular day a neighborhood woman was wandering through the cornfield wringing her hands and crying. She couldn't find her little boy and thought he must be hiding among the cornstalks. Mom asked could he have gone to the water, but the woman said he would never do that, he knew better. Mom sent me down the road to another house to call the First Aid just in case. I told the people in the house what was going on and they made the call for me. This was back in the days before cell phones. Anyway I ran and when I got back to the cornfield my Mother was busy keeping the lady from going down to the water as she could not swim and said her little boy could not swim. Mom made all the other kids stay in the car, but I ran down the path to the water.

As soon as I got to where I could see the sunshine on the water I saw the little boy lying on the bottom in about four or five feet. I could swim and started wading in to try and get him when over the bank came several members of the First Aid squad. They asked if I found him and I said yes, but they were calling for me to stay still and they would get him out. I waded back to the rocky creek bank. When they brought him up out of the water he was already dead, but they tried very hard to revive him. He had bubbles of foam coming out of his mouth. It was a sight I will never forget.

I attended his funeral. His Mother thanked and thanked me and told everyone how I found her boy even though it was too late.

It was months before I could slide my legs down between the sheets on my bed at night. It felt like I was going in the water and didn't know what I would touch down there. Although I did go swimming again later that year I would not go down and touch bottom for the same reason. I was afraid someone else might be on the bottom of the creek. I would dive in on one side and swim across and climb out on the other bank before I would put my feet down.

I still think about it sometimes if I am swimming where I can't see bottom.

HAPPY FATHERS DAY, DADDY!

When I remember I remember when my Dad passed` away and I wrote the following for him.

My Father will be spending his first Father's Day in heaven this year. I would like to tell you a little about his journey. You need to understand that everyone has always said my Dad would never be dead as long as I am alive because I am so much like him. And I guess I've always been somewhat of a Daddy's girl. He served in WWII and was gone several years when I was very small. After he came home he never had to spank me. No matter what I did or how badly I misbehaved he would just look at me and say, "I guess I'll go back in that old army again." And I would straighten right up. I didn't ever want him leaving again.

My Father was not a church going man , but he always made sure Moma had the car when it was time to go to service and I always went with her. And there was no use in me asking him if I could do something "worldly" because if Moma said it was wrong, then it was wrong.

When I was twelve years old I was to spend the day with my cousins after church. The family consisted of six boys and one girl so there was always a lot of give and take and sometimes it was not so friendly. This particular Sunday my aunt had not gone to church. The preacher had spoken quite vividly about heaven and hell. I felt a real stirring in my heart to accept Christ as my Savior, but knew that my Father was not a Christian and so did not go forward that day.

As we got out of the car and went into my Aunt's house I was crying. My Aunt immediately came to my rescue thinking one of the boys had hit me or taken something away from me. Through my sobs I said," I don't want to go to heaven if Daddy isn't going to be there."

As I got a little older and the Lord kept dealing with me I realized I had to make my own choice to accept Christ no matter what anyone else did. Thus began almost forty two years of praying earnestly for my Father. Every church I attended I would request prayer and have his name added to the prayer list. Many others in our family, including my Mother, were doing the same thing. Daddy only went to church on a few occasions during this entire time. He lived a good moral life and when he saw s church member doing something not quite right he always commented.

In January 1995 Daddy was diagnosed with lung cancer. He had a third of one lobe removed. Radiation treatments were also recommended. He received thirty four treatments in a hospital sixty five miles from home. Neighbors and friends helped drive him back and forth and I was there as much as possible. He would get so weak at times that we would get a motel room and stay over.

During one of our stay overs my parents were in one motel room and my husband and I in the adjoining room. Dad's appetite was already beginning to leave him and we were trying hard to tempt him with all kinds of good food. I went to their room early to see what I could get him for breakfast. I could tell from the redness of my Mother's eyes that they had been talking seriously. Daddy said he couldn't eat a bite until he got everything in here (pointing to his chest) right. Thinking he meant the cancer I told him he had to eat to keep his strength up for the rest of the treatments and the Doctors were optimistic about his recovery. But, with tears in his eyes, he said he had to make things right with God.

That day after his treatment Dad was hospitalized again. Even though he felt better in his heart he was not satisfied. We called for a minister friend to come and counsel with him. It was hard for my Dad to believe salvation could be so simple.

Later my Dad testified about a dream he had in which he saw a set of hands stretching from a cloud and another set of hands reaching upwards. He knew it was God reaching down to him and he would cry every time he told the story over the next nine months.

My Father was truly gloriously saved. He witnessed to everyone he saw. He called former supervisors and co-workers to tell them there had been a change in his life. He was bedfast the last four months of his life, but wanted to have prayer holding hands with everyone who came to visit. He told us things we never even guessed, how when he would travel for the company he would always ask the Lord to protect him. And, how at night, he would say the only prayer he knew, "Now I lay me down to sleep."

My Dad went home to heaven January 30, 1996. He spent his last precious eight days in the hospital. My Mother, myself, my husband and his only grandson loved him to death. Many other family members and friends came during that time to say "goodbye" in their own way also.

While going through some papers etc. since his going home we found a hospital bracelet and a note in my Dad's handwriting in an album of his. The note said, "The hospital room where I found the Lord about March 15, 1995". My Mother has no idea when he put them among his things.

Last year for Father's Day I gave my Dad his first very own Bible with his name embossed in gold. This year I am sending him this letter with all my love and he is walking the streets of gold.

Author's parents, Clyde Traynem and Marie Eleanor Alfred Bell, The picture was published along with the article in the Pentecostal Holiness Church magazine in June 1996.

GALL BLADDER SURGERY

When I remember I remember when I had my first surgery. I was thirty eight years old and had been ill for eighteen months with episodes of nausea, vomiting and severe pain. Numerous tests were run in the Doctor's office and as an out patient at the hospital, but a cause could not be found. The Dr. I was going to decided all my symptoms were all in my mind, just a bad case of nerves, so he prescribed Valium four times a day. I took two pills and quickly decided if I took the medicine as prescribed I would be a zombie. I also did not believe my problem was nerves.

After one particularly bad episode I ended up at the emergency room. The Dr. listened to my story, checked me over and said, "I don't know what is wrong with you, but I do believe something is and we are going to find it". He admitted me to the hospital and started running tests. I was there a week and they did everything possible, but still nothing presented itself so I was discharged.

I continued having the episodes and several months later was admitted to the hospital again. The tests were redone, but before they were all completed I became jaundiced. The Dr. was elated because he felt they finally had a clue to the problem. They did a liver biopsy late one evening and I became violently ill. I began throwing up mouthful after mouthful of vile green bile. Surgery was scheduled for the next morning, but all night I pleaded with them to take me earlier. During surgery they found one gall stone, so small it never showed up on any of the tests, but finally moved and blocked the duct from the gall bladder to the liver and caused the jaundice.

For several days after the surgery I was in a semi-conscious state. My family hired a private duty nurse for the night shift and family members were with me around the clock, a touch and go situation.

Two things from this experience stand out especially. After I began showing signs of improvement my husband went back to the Dr. who had first treated me for over a year. When it came his turn to be seen, the Dr. asked why he was there. My husband said, "I just came to tell you my wife was operated on for her nerves and almost died". I think at that point the Dr. almost had a heart attack. "What are you talking about? You can't be operated on for nerves."

"Well, you said that was what was wrong and she just had surgery so that had to be what it was for."

The second thing that stands out in my memory is that on the morning of my surgery the last thing my husband said to me as they were rolling me down the hall was "The Lord is my Shepherd". I was in the hospital two weeks after the surgery, but it was three months before I had strength enough to go back to church. The pastor did not know what my husband had whispered to me and he certainly did not know I would be in church that Sunday. Yet, his sermon was Psalm 23; The Lord is my Shepherd.

So, when I remember I remember when God took me through the valley of the shadow of death. How wonderful He is to me!

MY DREAM

When I remember I remember when I had a life changing dream several years ago. I had been facing some very real, very serious battles in my life, battles I couldn't win, battles with only one conclusion unless God miraculously intervened. I didn't want to share the nature of those battles with anyone and am still not ready to do that. But I tried to win them or at least deal with them on my own.

In doing so I made some good decisions and some bad. But slowly and surely my joy and peace drained away. I prayed daily for help and daily had to say "I'm sorry" to someone and ask for God's help and forgiveness again.

But on this night, December 26, 2007, I went to bed, went to sleep and had a most vivid dream. I was in my car, by myself, traveling up what was a little hill, but which quickly became steeper and steeper. There were other vehicles on the road, but I didn't pay any special attention to them. Just before I reached the crest of the hill traffic ahead of me stopped. I couldn't see a reason, but applied my brakes and came to a complete stop with no trouble.

But something was wrong with my brakes and they wouldn't hold. I pumped and pumped the brake pedal. I pushed it all the way to the floor and stood on it holding it as tight as I could, but the car started slipping backwards.

I was slipping backwards slowly at first, still pumping the brakes, trying to steer between and around the vehicles behind me. But gathering speed and more speed, all the time wrestling with the steering wheel and brakes and calling out to God for His help. I could actually feel my arms and shoulders getting tired and hurting from the effort. My neck was hurting from turning my head trying to see where to steer.

Then I woke up and was awake a long time. I tried to pray, but was so tired and sleepy I couldn't so finally went back to sleep. I dreamed the exact same dream again. And again woke up, stayed awake a long while and went back to sleep for the third time that night. For the third time I dreamed the same dream only this time instead of waking up at the same point the dream continued.
By this time I was really careening down the hill. I knew I was either going to run off the side of the road over the embankment or crash into someone else coming behind me. Finally I said," Lord, You have to help me stop this car. My arms are getting so tired I can't fight this wheel much longer. I can't see to steer around all these other vehicles on the road and the brakes still won't work. This car is completely out of my control now".

Still I kept going backward at a high rate of speed. Then I said, Lord, You have to get in the driver's seat. It's Your car now" and I slid over to the passenger side of the car. "I'm only a passenger from now on. I don't know exactly where I am, I don't know how high this mountain is. I don't know how many valleys or rivers I have to cross, but I do know my final destination and with You in control I can make it safely to heaven".

I have a peace in my heart that I have not had in some time and I believe God will renew my joy as I leave the driving to Him. Several times since my dream I have been tempted to forge ahead, but was checked by the Holy Spirit and would just look up and say,

"Lord, You are in the driver's seat now".

HOG BUTCHERING

*W*hen I remember I remember when it would be hog butchering time in the fall. My Grandma would always raise four or five hogs to butcher for the meat to have in the winter. My Dad was the chief butcher, but always had help from other family members. I remember they would start early in the morning. My Dad would shoot the hog with his rifle. He was a good shot and I never remember an animal suffering. I can hear all the animal rights people today arguing that point. But I kinda feel it was more important for people to use what God provided to feed their families.

Grandma would have huge kettles of water boiling over an outside fire. After the hog had been gutted to remove the intestines etc. it would be hung on a tripod made of poles. The hog would be dipped in and out of the hot water until the skin with all the hair could be scraped away.

After the hog was fully cleaned it would be cut into hams and shoulders. Parts would be made into sausage. My Grandma would salt cure the meat by putting table salt thickly over the entire piece and hanging it in the smokehouse until cured. She used the meat all winter and always seemed to have plenty.

I remember the first time I went to Cass, West Virginia to visit my boyfriend's grandmother. She thought I was really a city girl all the way from Covington, Virginia. She was slicing a ham to fix for dinner and said to me that she guessed I had never seen anything like that. To which I replied, "Oh, yes. My grandmother has a whole smokehouse full of hams". Then his grandmother just thought I was a smart aleck kid!

HALLOWEEN

When I remember I remember when you could go Trick or Treat by yourself or with a group of friends and didn't have to worry about the "bad guys" getting you. I remember when you could stop at every house whether you knew the people or not....when small town Main Street would be blocked off and all the kids could run around and show off their costumes. And I remember that almost without fail the costumes were homemade and you were only limited by your imagination as to what you would be.

I remember when my Dad would give out double handfuls of candy to each "Tricker" and easily spend $50.00 on candy when it was a lot less expensive than it is now. I remember when the lady who was to become my future mother-in-law made fudge and wrapped each piece in wax paper. Kids came from everywhere to get a piece of that fudge.

I remember when the meanest trick of all was to put soap on someone's car windows.

I remember wishing for my children and grandchildren the return to simpler happier times when you didn't have to worry about things like razor blades in apples and rat poison in candy; when you didn't have to go have your bag of treats x-rayed before you could eat them. A time when you didn't have to worry about automobiles being overturned and set on fire, windows broken instead of soaped. A time when everyone didn't have to dress like the hottest star around and when all those costumes were sold the parents wouldn't give in to the tantrums and pay exorbitant prices to keep their child from being the oddball.

I remember being thankful for my simple childhood....and sad to know it would never be that stress free for my family.

A WAR CHRISTMAS

When I remember I remember when I was very small during WWII. My Mother and I stayed with my Great grandparents and Grandmother while my dad was overseas. I remember one Christmas when we were there. Money of course was tight and it was hard to find anything to purchase. Everything was going into the war effort.

That year my aunt, uncle, their two girls and three boys were also at Grandma's to spend Christmas. Somehow the parents were able to buy three little dolls, identical except for the color of their dresses. One was in blue, one in pink and one in yellow. My Grandmother's sofa had three cushions. Santa Claus left my things on one cushion and my girl cousins gifts on the other cushions. I believe I got the doll with the blue dress. One little pile for each of us although the only thing I remember is the dolls. I have no idea what the boys got or where it was placed. Maybe they really did get the lump of coal.

Today the kids have absolutely everything and still want more. It is sad to me to know they would never be content with my Christmas from back then, but with the little doll and my imagination I had hours of fun and memories which linger today.

There is a doll among my Mother's things today which has a cracked face and is now dressed in a green crocheted dress. I wonder if it is the doll I remember and she kept it all these years for me.

BROKEN SANTA SLEIGH

When I remember I remember when I was about five or six years old. It was just before Christmas and Moma and I were shopping at one of the five and dime stores in Covington, Virginia. She was buying some Christmas candy. Back then the candy was not prepackaged, but displayed in glass cases in the store. You told the clerk what you wanted and how much and they weighed it out for you and put it into a little paper bag.

Other small items for sale were displayed on top of the cases. This particular day there was a small, maybe five or six inch Santa in a white sleigh pulled by six little white deer held together by green ribbon. I was told not to touch, but I tried to reach up to the top of the counter anyway and knocked the sleigh off. Two of the reindeer broke so the clerk told my Mother she would have to pay. My Mother made me carry the purchase home as punishment. I was crying all the way, but doubt if I ever broke anything in the store again.

Sixty years later I found that sleigh still packed in the original box marked .59 cents. I now put it out each year at Christmas and tell all the children and grandchildren how I came to have it. But I do set it up on the shelf where they can't knock it off.

A CHRISTMAS TO REMEMBER

When I remember I remember the year I was twelve years old. All I wanted for Christmas was a real ladies watch. Not a children's watch, but a watch with a small petite face and a gold colored stretch band.

It was several days before Christmas and we were on our way to Grandma Bells. I was setting in the back seat on the drivers side behind my Dad. He was watching me in the rear view mirror, but I didn't know that.

He explained to me that money was very tight and they couldn't get me the watch I wanted for Christmas. But maybe they could get it for me for my birthday in June. I was so disappointed I cried, but very softly so they wouldn't hear and I told him I understood.

Christmas morning came and Mom handed me a shoebox all wrapped up. When I opened the box there was the most beautiful ladies watch you've ever seen. I was so happy I cried again.

Daddy explained that if I had thrown a fit when I thought I wasn't getting the watch I really wouldn't have. And he meant every word.

A life lesson well taught and well learned.

Today I have a 14 karat ladies watch that my husband gave me for Christmas one year which I love. But it still doesn't mean as much as the one I received all those years ago.

CHRISTMAS SCHEDULE

When I remember I remember when my Dad came home from WWII and we had a family schedule for Christmas every year. We would get up at our home and see what Santa brought and open our gifts. Then we would get ready and I could pick out one or two things to take with me to play with all day.

My aunt, uncle and seven cousins only lived one mile from us. My Grandparents lived in the house next to them. We always went to my Uncle's for breakfast. My aunt was so use to cooking for a lot of people that a few more didn't matter at all. I would show my cousins what I had and see what Santa brought them. After I got older Mom would help me gather up toys etc. that I had in good condition and didn't play with and we would slip them in with Santa's gifts for the cousins. Sometimes I would be asked to give away something I really wanted even though I didn't play with it much and I always did. My parents were determined I would not grow up to be an only selfish child.

After breakfast we would go to my Grandma Bell's which was about forty miles away and the weather didn't matter. For years I was the only grandchild. They were tenant farmers and had very little cash so I never remember a store bought gift from them. But Grandma had a big Anchor Hocking baking dish with a lid and it was filled to the top with all kinds of Christmas candy. I nibbled all day while we were there. After my Dad's brothers and sisters were old enough to work they always got me nice things and I always had more than enough. Grandma always had a big dinner. My favorite things were the mashed potatoes (made with a wooden potato masher) with gobs of home made butter and the homemade applesauce cake made with caramel frosting. No worry about cholesterol in those days. (Grandma Bell always let me eat with a big spoon and I still do that to this day.)

Then, back to Covington and the evening meal with another aunt, uncle and cousins there. After that, it was back home, sleepy, tired, stomach full and ready for bed. I guess I really did sleep and dream of sugar plums.

POETRY

WHIMSICAL

WHEN I REMEMBER

When I remember, I remember when
I once was young
I once was thin.
People said, "Don't worry,
It won't last
All good things eventually pass."

And it must be true because
I'm no longer young
I'm no longer thin
But still when I remember,
I remember when
And in my memory
I am.

WANNABE

I love to read, I only try to write,
My house is a mess, my hair is a fright.
No time to vacuum, no time to chase rust
Getting thoughts on paper right now is a must.

Patterson, Kellerman, Sanders I'm not
I forget to cross t's and fail to dot
However it's fun and I enjoy every minute
And with luck some day I may write a sonnet.

Until then laugh, make fun if you must
I'll still set here with my book amidst all of my dust.

STAR LIGHT

Star light, star bright
How I wish I could see you tonight
To hear your voice, to see your smile
Forget my cares and worries awhile.

Time goes so slowly when we are apart
You truly are the beat of my heart
Each waking moment my thoughts are of you
And my sweetest dreams all the night through.

If you can't come to me
I'll come where you are
And the rest of our days
We'll wish on the same star.

SKIP

Skip, skip, skip to my Lou,
You love me and I love you.
Life could be so carefree and gay
It shouldn't be any other way.

Yet there are days so cloudy and grey
The sun won't shine come what may.
But the darker it gets, the easier to stay
Focused on your love to guide my way.

I see sunshine and green meadows ahead
I see you sleeping beside me in my bed.
I see bluebirds, flowers and rainbows
I don't deserve it everyone knows,
But I'm happier than I have a right to be
And also because you came skipping to me.

WINDOW SHOPPING

I went to the mall today
To see who I could see
My friend said actually I went
So they could all see me.

Maybe she's right, maybe she's wrong
I really don't care
I just felt a need in my life
To go somewhere.

Browsing through the stores I could pretend
I was really in Italy with a friend
Or maybe France or Spain por favore
I really can't ask for anything more.

Than a few hours to look
Through a travel catalog
Or sip cappuccino or drink an eggnog.
My heart lightens, my spirits soar
Just to be me, just to go to the store.

I think I will buy some bright yellow jeans
With a red halter top, would that mean
I could go back and be sixteen?

Oh, no! Never again
I'll just give the clothes
To my granddaughter's best friend.

Then they will laugh and giggle at me
And I will laugh at them
For you see
Age is in the mind and not in the knee.

MOUSE IN THE HOUSE

Oh, no! There's a mouse in the house
Where did it go, where can it be?
I can tell you right now
There's not enough room here for it and for me.

Dig the car from the snow
So to Walmart I can go
Mouse traps, D-Con, what else can I see
This house is too small for both the mouse and me.

Set cheese out as bait, peanut butter too
Tell me quick, what else can I do?
I could get a cat, maybe even two
What a dilemma, what to do, what to do?

I'll go to bed, but won't sleep a wink
Until I hear that trap go clink
Yea, I heard it, let me go see,
The first trap got it- he's dead as can be.

Now comes the Lysol, the Clorox and such
I use it while listening to PETA folks fuss
How cruel to snuff out the little ones life
Pardon me, you sound a lot like my wife.

FAMILY OCCASIONS AND FAMILY

HAPPY 50ᵀᴴ BIRTHDAY!

I'll never forget my first sight of you
It's the day I fell in love
Your eyes scrunched so tight
Seven lbs, 21 inches, bald
Spidery arms and legs hanging out from the nurses' hands
You were beautiful
You were mine.

Fearless, brave
All boy from the start
But loving, thoughtful
For a Mother's heart.

Your Dad's hunting buddy
My helper in every way
I never wished
One minute away.

I worried about you
Nagged I'm sure
You never wanted to pick up
Your clothes from the floor.

Honest in all things
Truthful and fair
You're still beautiful
A Son beyond compare.

Nothing has changed
Months and years have come and gone
You're no longer a boy,
But you're still my son.

No words can express
My love and my pride
But in my heart
It will always abide.

25TH ANNIVERSARY

I fell in love with your blue eyes
And you fell in love with my eyes of brown
I think we knew right from the start
We would never let each other down.

The days and weeks and months and years
Have gone so swiftly by
We've laughed and loved and worked and played
And sometimes had to cry.

The problems have come
And the problems have gone
But we never had to face them alone.

You've been my strength
I've been your shield
Taking turns we would both have to yield
You had your way
I had mine
For 25 years it has worked just fine.

I'm looking forward to the coming years too
My only desire is to spend them with you
Forever and always, never to part
For you alone hold the keys to my heart.

50TH ANNIVERSARY

50 years have come and gone
Since we first said I do
It's hard to believe the time has past
Because when I look at you.

I still see the strong young man
With hair so thick and brown
The heart so true, the love so strong
I knew would never let me down.

Just as in our vows
You promised you would stay
Close beside me to provide and care
In each and every way.

And you have been there
No matter what the cost
In many times and situations
Without you I would have been lost.

You have allayed my fears
And dried my tears
And held my hand when I was ill.
You've laughed with me and at me
But I love you still.

I have counted on your presence
On your strength and on your love
And every day am thankful
To our Heavenly Father above

For He has kept us and blest us
Each and every day
And if I could go back again
I would say I do again
Only to you again.

GRADUATION

I've always said
Reach for that star
I know you can
It's not too far.

You can do anything
You set your mind to
And I will be here
To encourage you.

Go on and dream
For things good and true
Work for that goal
That is set just for you.

If it's worth having
It's worth working for
And will be appreciated
All that much more.

Never use the words
I wish or I should
But when you look back
Say I knew I could.

And when your day is over
And twilight starts to fall
You will have no regrets
But thankfulness for all.

THANK YOU!

Thank you for coming
You don't know what it meant
The gift of your presence
Was truly heaven sent!

CHILDREN

You may not have been planned
But you were wanted
You may have been spanked
But you were loved
We've always known
That you were a gift
To us
From our Father above.

SON AND DAUGHTERS

Son and daughters, I love you so much
I pray for you daily, but in God I must trust.

He promised to keep that which was committed to Him
He gave you to me and said take care of them.

I've tried to live the life before you
And in all things been honest and true.

By my example more than my word
Hoping through the Spirit it would be heard.

My time is growing shorter, my days will soon end
I leave you in the hands of my Savior and Friend

Please meet me there on the golden shore
And we will praise Jesus forevermore.

Your sons and daughters I will be looking for too
But they need to see an example in you.

Don't let my life have been lived in vain
I need to know I will see you again.

Bring up a child in the way he should go
And he will not depart from it when he gets old.

I will see you in heaven I believe in my heart
Only a short time will we be apart.

So love me and miss me a little if you must,
But most important of all in God put your trust.

From top to bottom, Theodore Clyde Moore, Susan Elizabeth Moore Shifflett, Anne Marie Moore Martin.

FAMILY

I love you each one
So very much
Wish we could be closer
So I could touch
Your hand and let you know
I'm here for you
It's always been so
I've watched you grow
I've felt your pain
I've seen your joy
And felt young again
You're part of me
I hope the good
Will stay with you forever
As it should.

MOMA'S HAIR

It's thinning now
Patches of scalp showing through
White as cotton,
Beautiful!
Worn like a crown!

MOM

My earthly home has gone away
I just laid my mother to rest
Of all the mothers in the world
She truly was the best.

I know that she is happy now
And free from care and pain
And most importantly than that
I shall see her again.

Together we shall walk
Upon that golden shore
With all our loved ones and friends
Who have gone on before.

God Himself shall wipe
The tears from our eyes
And we will live forever
With Him in the skies.

ONLY LOVE

My mind swims with thoughts of
Sparkling chocolate eyes
Topped with thick wavy mahogany hair
Lips curved upward in anticipation
Of the journey ahead.

Not knowing where it would lead
But hopeful, enthusiastic, confident
That rivers could be crossed and
Mountains climbed
Arm in arm, Heart to heart.

Now one son, two daughters, fifty years
Rivers have been crossed
Mountains have been climbed
My mind swims with thoughts of
My young love, my old love, my only love!

Theodore (Ted) Roosevelt Moore, Jr.

MISCELLANEOUS TOPICS
AND POETRY STYLES

BASEBALL

There it lay in the middle of the floor
In plain sight
No one seemed to know how it got there
Or take ownership for its flight.
The jagged opening lets in cold air
And frosts slivers of glass
Slippers had to be found
Before dust pan and broom
Who will pay? Why was it thrown?
In this direction, into this room?
Did they know who lived here?
Did they care?
A peck on the door, mystery solved,
A little boy about four to collect the
Ball for big brother.

TIME FOR ME

I never have a minute
To really call my own.
Come here, do that
What's taking you so long?

You don't do things
The way you should
Because you don't do them
The way I would.

Would, Should, Could
How happy I would be
If only you would let me
Just be me!

SESTINA

The needles flash in and out
Weaving the strands of silver
And gold into a work of art.
Each thread a pattern of its own
To be a gift to others, but more
To myself.

Soothing, comforting gifts of warmth
The threads go to friends, strangers,
Family too, in shades of silver
And gold to delight the eyes.
The needles fly, but the best of all
Is the time for myself to help.

A hat, scarf or mittens, gifts to the lonely
Homeless selves on the corner
Where the fire in the barrel catches the silver
Or gold glint
Of the thread and flashes it back like a mirror
And the needles keep clacking.

Myself with no hair due to cancers ravage
Now head covered with a gift of love
Made with silver and red
Gold and green
All threads woven together
With flash of needles.

Each gift different, yet the same
How many threads does it take to
Make a golden scarf
Or silver hat?
Must work faster to complete the gifts so I
Can deliver them myself.

In and out, row after row the needles
Hook the thread. Now this pattern,
Now that, golden visions in my head
Turn to silver objects in my hand.
As the gifts are given the smiles of
Excitement returned will be my self satisfaction.

The gift of self I give away
With each gold and silver offering
All it takes is needle and thread.

WHAT WILL YOU DO?

What will you do now?

The heat is so intense I have to cover my mouth and nose
Breathe through a wet handkerchief
Hardly one stone left on another
Red embers carried on the night wind.

Call for more help
Pray, thankful to be alive
Help my neighbor with his nightmare
Pass refreshments to all who fight.

What will I do? Start over. There is nothing else.

BUFFALO SPRING

Some might call it a diamond, but I would say it was still uncut, certainly not polished. Set in a bowl, ringed by snow tipped mountain peaks, small slate stream cascading by. Brilliant blue sky, evergreens vivid against spotty snow patches, ground carpeted with needles. Five hundred twelve called it home, others drifting through with the seasons change. Maybe a thousand at fall jamboree. Regulars were outlying ranchers coming in for supplies when the wagons from back east were due. Unkempt, rough, solitary miners to find out the worth of a single nugget or small pouch of dust harvested from the stream. Trappers come to trade their beaver hides for another stake to make it through the long cold isolated winter in the high mountains. They slept at the Buffalo Wallow and paid dearly for their yearly bath at the livery. Cheap whiskey was available at the Silver Dollar where the piano blasted out rowdy songs barely heard over the noise of bottles clinking and disputed card games and the girls enticing them to spend the last coins they had for the year. Sometimes, they would go to MOMS for a home cooked meal prepared on a real stove instead of over a campfire, but more often than not they went to see red headed Suzy who served their buffalo stew and hot biscuits. She was almost as pretty as the girls at the Silver Dollar. An occasional Indian family or small tribe passed the trading post and left bone implements and deer hides and took white man's blankets and knives in exchange. They were warily watched and rarely welcomed. Buffalo Spring, Wyoming. Where have all the buffalo gone?

COOPERATION

Cooperation
What a word
What does it mean
Have you heard?

To work together
For the common good
Oh, how I wish
That you would!

FOUND POETRY

A locked suitcase full of pretty cosmetic things
Opened by a gold key
Bottle after bottle, jar after jar
Fragrance like incense.

Chinaberry flowers, oh, no!
Secret ingredients, try
Flaming paint on her mouth
Only two dollars.

My husband keeps the money
An old man, I wouldn't ask for anything.

FROM NIGHT TO DAY

Then, born into the squalor and dirt I remember the noise and chaos of the concrete jungle, the graffiti on the cinder block walls, the skinny, snarling dogs and hissing cats at war with the humans as they pawed through the overflowing garbage cans to get the last roach infested scrap before the rats.

Now, pulled by boot strings to this quiet, peaceful place of well kept green lawns, looking out at the birds on the feeder, squirrels and rabbits frolicking in the yard and deer coming from the woods at night to nibble on the flowers and vegetables so lovingly tended in the day.

Then, broken glass everywhere, people huddled in small groups on four by four peeling concrete stoops for slight relief from oppressive heat. Smells of boiling cabbage wafting from inside. Children, wet, dirty, half clothed, crying. Mothers, cigarette dangling from lips, yelling. Watching passers by from the corners of their eyes. Fathers appearing when welfare checks come. Another baby on the way, more money.

Now, ensconced on thickly padded lounge on shaded deck, laughing children splashing in pool. Smell of steak on grill. Glancing through magazine lying on lap, mostly soaking up rays of golden sunlight. Waving to neighbors. Car in driveway, father home from work.

GONE

"He's gone."
"Gone? Where could he go? Have you looked for him?"
"No, I mean he's dead."
The words hit me like a blow to the head.

How could it be?
I just spoke to him a few days ago
I found a jacket he brought to me
When he came home from Korea.

I took a picture with my grandson wearing it,
Mailed it with his Christmas card
Hoping he would remember still
But he may already have been too ill.

How do you close out eighty years on this earth?
By remembering the good times
By letting the bad times fade into the past
The loving memories will always last.

INTERNAL RHYME

One thing we know as we go along is that we all have trouble and woe. But what sets us apart from the crowd is how we feel in our heart. Are we happy or sad, accepting the good and the bad? Climbing the mountains, sharing the load with others traveling the same road. Knowing together we can conquer the way and come out on top to savor the day of sunshine, blue skies, gentle breezes and smiling brown eyes.

LITTLE JO

It all started so long ago
When Dad would call me his "little Jo".
Party dresses gave way to torn blue jeans.
Mascara never brought out my blue eyes.
I had no interest in those kinds of things.

Moma tried, she ranted and raved
When I wanted my brother's guns
Instead of my sister's doll.
Dad just smiled, stoked his pipe,
Said "Hang tough".

I signed up for two, that should be enough
I'll get some college paid for,
Maybe be a teacher,
Maybe a nurse,
At least go back to wearing skirts.

I paraded and trained
Dropped and gave ten
Saluted and "Yes, Sired"
With the best of the men.
And felt like I was better than them.

The glass ceiling shattered,
It really cracked
And never did I
Seriously look back,
But reenlisted again and again.

Dad still calls me his "little Jo".
He is so proud
I have come this far,
But I won't stop
'till I get the fifth star.

LOST PERSON AND PLACE

He always had a pipe between his teeth, helped keep his
Hands busy relighting,
The smell of Half and Half clinging to his skin and clothes. Tiny
Holes burnt by falling embers
Even in his suits. How she fussed about that!

Graduated from barber school on GI bill. Cut my hair, then
went to town on Saturday night.
"Bob tailing" he would call it, sticking out his index finger for me
To hold on while we visited
Up and down the busy sidewalk. Took his last dime to buy me
A comic book.

His pride in me no greater than my pride in him. Two of a kind
everyone said.

RELIGIOUS

MORNING PRAYER

Lord, give me strength for another day,
Help for my work and a time for play.

I'm grateful to You for all You have done,
Most of all for giving the world Your Son.

I'm so human that often I grumble and complain,
But inside I know how fortunate I am.

For You are my Savior, my Friend and my Lord
To be in heaven with You will be my reward.

Rest for my body, peace for my soul
Only then will the full story be told.

How You've kept me and guided every day of my life,
And protected from evil and all manner of strife.

Help me to be more thankful today
A blessing to those along my way.

A worthy vessel to be used by You
In all that I say and all that I do.

GOLIATHS

Do you have a Goliath in your life?
Well, I do.
I have one, maybe even two
And sometimes three.
And not a day goes by that at least one of them
Doesn't throw out a challenge to me.

And I cannot face those calls
I have no idea what to do
Except to hold on and believe that
Lord, You do.

My patience is tried
My wisdom is small
Thank You, Jesus
That You have it all.
And will give to me
What I need
At the right time
And in the amount needed
To cover the problem
And help me come out
Victorious in You, Lord
Forever more
Until I thank You in person
On heaven's bright shore.

WALK THE VALLEY

When I walk through the valley, I won't have to go alone.
When I see the shadows lengthen, I'll just know I'm closer home.
Part of me wants to stay here, part of me wants to go.
Loved ones and friends on both sides
Are calling for me, don't you know?

ROCKY ROAD

Lord, I don't like this path
You've put me on
It's way too dark
And far too long.
The path is rocky
The way is steep
My steps are slow
My back is weak.
I'm not sure
Which way to go
But in my heart I know
My final end
Will be in Heaven with You
My Savior, my Friend.

FALTERING AND SLOW

Lord, my legs are weak
My steps faltering and slow
Oft times now it seems
I cannot go.

But 2000 years ago
You looked ahead
You saw me today
And the path I tred.

You took an extra stripe
It was just for me
And if I believe
I will be set free.

Give me the strength I need
To do what has to be done
Give me the faith
To believe in Thy Son.

I thank You today
For whatever must be
So that I may rest
Eternally with Thee.

I'VE SEEN GOD

I've seen God. I really have. I've seen God. Actually I have to shut my eyes real tight or I would see Him everyday, but I have seen God.

In the spring I watch the birds darken the blue of the sky. I see the flowers push their heads through the ground. I see the joy on the faces of passersby as they enjoy the warm sunshine.

In the summer I watch the calves frolic in the field. I see the breeze blowing the weeping willow tree. And I watch the first timers at the beach as they run into and out of the waves, squealing with excitement.

In the fall I watch the birds gather for their long flight back to their winter home. I see the beautiful harvest of the golden pumpkins, corn and apples. And I watch the children waiting on the school bus.

In the quiet of the winter I see the deer come to the water's edge to drink. I see the snow cover the barren ground with its soft blanket of white. And I see the wonder anew on each face as they remember "Peace on earth".

Yes, I've seen God.

Thank you, Lord, for all you've shown me and make me open and receptive to all those sights I've missed.

CHRISTMAS

We have seen His star
And traveled far
To worship Him
Beautiful Babe of Bethlehem.

ILLNESS

ALZHEIMER'S

My heart breaks a little more each day
As I watch what you do and hear what you say,
I know you're slipping far, far away
And I can't go with you or even get you to stay
Here with me yet awhile, but oh, to hold you close
And see your sweet smile and know that you love me
With all that is you and hope you remember
That I love you too.

The older we get the more aware we become
Of all the things that happen to separate us from
Those nearest and dearest, our very meaning in life
You were meant as my husband and I as your wife.
And when you no longer remember my name,
Just hold my hand and know I'll still love you the same
As through that dark tunnel you go

I'll remember your love, comfort and strength
And I want you to know
I'll be there for you
As you have always been here for me.
Forever, my Darling, until eternity.

TUNNEL AHEAD

I've started down that dark tunnel
Where there is no light at the end
But I ask one thing before I go
Will you still be my friend?

When I can no longer remember your name
Will you still remember me?
And smile and laugh at the things that were
And how we used to be.

Don't dwell too long on what is now
The good outweighs the bad
And if I could have one final wish
It would be; please don't be sad.

Life has its ups and downs you know
We have our share of woe
But we have a Heavenly Father
To keep us as we go.

There would be things I would change
If I could do it again
But I would never ever change
Having you for my friend

So, stroke my hair and hold my hand
Even though you don't understand
There are no answers I can give
But my advice is
To your fullest....LIVE!!

SONNET

Swiftly the days and years go by
Time is flying away
I need to work harder to try
And convince you to stay.
If you leave, my life will end
How could I go on?
You are my love, also my friend
I don't want to be alone.
Don't let the memory loss
Take you away from me
Hold on, Fight, whatever the cost
You have to help, don't you see?
Don't cry for what you've lost, but smile for what you've had,
The good in our life together, far outweighs the bad.

HAIKU

A Japanese form of poetry from the seventeenth century. Each verse tells a story with the first line being five syllables, the second line being seven syllables and the third line being five syllables.

NIGHT SKY

Cobalt canopy
Dazzling pinpoints of bright light
Majestic night sky

YOU STILL HAVE YOUR COW

LIFE

Neighbor dead, house torched
Deputy shot, on run for life
You still have your cow.

LIBERTY

Until they squeeze you
Into small jail cell for life
Is it worth it now?

PURSUIT

No more to visit
Over fence post and barbwire
Through glass, no touching

HAPPINESS

Gentle breezes skimming
Face tilted up to suns rays
Memories remain.

BROKEN BONE

Turned too quickly, fell
Feet tangled with footstool, lost
Balance, heard arm pop.

Shoulder, elbow, wrist
What hurts most? Can't really say
Waiting for x-ray.

Right arm and shoulder
Weeks of therapy ahead
Be more careful now.

THE HUNT

In woods before day
Excitement builds in tree stand
Hope buck comes this way

Waiting patiently
Twig snaps announcing presence
Magnificent sight.

Eyes meet, nostrils flare
Salutes, graceful antler sweep
Twirls, melts into mist.

WINTER SNOW

Snow falling softly
Most beautiful time of year
Inside looking out.

Bundled in warm suits
Children making snow angels
Stand out against sky

Snowmen with coal eyes
And carrot nose with twig arms
Stand guard over night

Sunshine melts away
All the labor of the day
Memories remain

MALL SANTA

Arms laden with bags
Pushing, shoving to and fro
Missing Christmas joy

Long expected wait
In line to see Santa Claus
Fat old man, white beard

No time to listen
Carols playing intercom
Just loud background noise

Late lunch, missed naptime
Smiling eyes turned to tears
Need to go home now

Be good, Santa watches
Do it all again next year
Hope more Christmas cheer.